POSITIVE BEHAVIOR
FOR
MINECRAFTERS
AN UNOFFICAL GUIDE

50 Fun Activities to Help Kids Manage Emotions

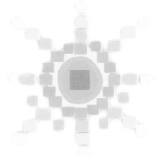

ERIN FALLIGANT

Sky Pony Press
New York, New York

Copyright © 2022 by Hollan Publishing, Inc.

Minecraft® is a registered trademark of Notch Development AB.

The Minecraft game is copyright © Mojang AB.

Minecraft® is a registered trademark of Notch Development AB. The Minecraft game is copyright © Mojang AB.

Visit our website at www.skyponypress.com.

10 9 8 7 6 5 4 3 2 1

Library of Congress Cataloging-in-Publication Data is available on file.

Print ISBN: 978-1-5107-7251-9

Cover design by Brian Peterson
Interior design by Noora Cox
Cover illustration by Grace Sandford
Interior illustrations by Amanda Brack

Printed in China

DEAR MINECRAFTER,

Big feelings—they come and go like clouds in the sky. Everyone has stormy emotions sometimes. When they strike, it's *hard* to make good choices.

We can't control the feelings that pop up, but we can learn smart ways to calm down and keep our cool. We can figure out what we feel and what we need. And we can choose to act in ways that make things better, not worse.

This book will give you the tools you need to handle big feelings and get along better with family and friends. As you tackle fun challenges with your favorite Minecraft characters, you'll learn tricks to use in the *real* world too.

You can handle whatever feelings come your way at home, at school—anywhere! Ready to begin?

CONTENTS

SUNNY OR STORMY?

Some feelings are warm and peaceful, like sunshine. Others are strong and stormy. Feelings aren't "bad" or "good," but some emotions are stronger than others.

How do these emotions feel for you? Circle one answer for each.

1. When I'm **sad,** I feel . . .   **SUNNY** OR **STORMY**

2. When I'm **nervous,** I feel . . .   **SUNNY** OR **STORMY**

3. When I'm **happy,** I feel . . .   **SUNNY** OR **STORMY**

4. When I'm **mad,** I feel . . .   **SUNNY** OR **STORMY**

5. When I'm **jealous,** I feel . . .   **SUNNY** OR **STORMY**

6. When I'm **excited,** I feel . . .   **SUNNY** OR **STORMY**

7. When I'm **frustrated,** I feel . . . **SUNNY** OR **STORMY**

8. When I'm **scared,** I feel . . .   **SUNNY** OR **STORMY**

WHEN A STORM BREWS

You can tell when a storm is brewing in Minecraft. You can tell when your feelings grow stormy, too! Your cheeks might get hot. Your heart might pound. What else might you feel?

Write what you feel, then draw an arrow to where in the body you might feel it.

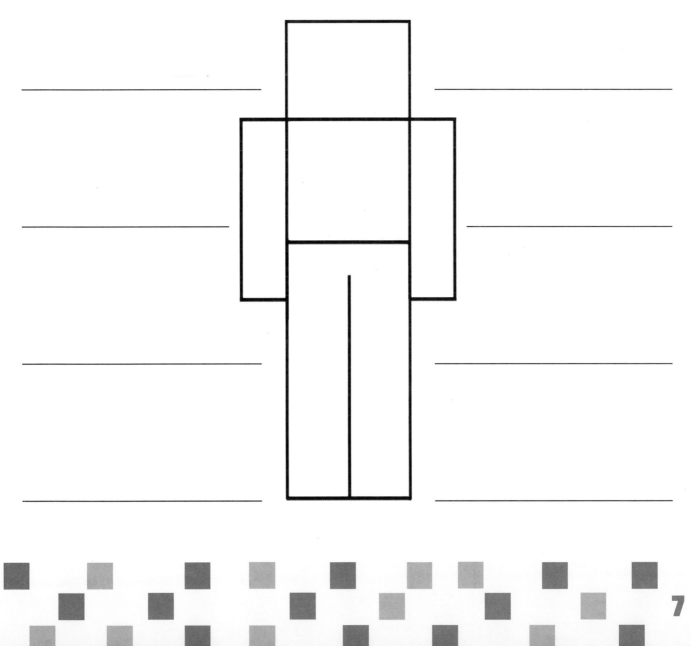

WHO'S THE BOSS?

When you have strong feelings, you might want to explode or hit something, just like a wither boss. Strong feelings are hard to control! But there's something you *can* control.

To find out what, circle each word that comes right after the word WITHER.

WITHER YOU WITHER CAN CAN'T WITHER CONTROL WITHER HOW WHEN WITHER YOU THEY WITHER ACT BEHAVE WITHER ON IN WITHER YOUR WITHER FEELINGS. WITHER YOU'RE STILL WITHER THE A WITHER BOSS SPIDER WITHER OF WITHER YOUR WEATHER WITHER BEHAVIOR.

Write the words you circled here:

_____

_____

_____

TRICKS AND TREASURES

When you have strong feelings, you can use little tricks to calm down. These tricks are as powerful as potions or enchantments. Keep them in your treasure chest for when you need them most.

Which tricks can you use to calm down? Rearrange the words below to find out.

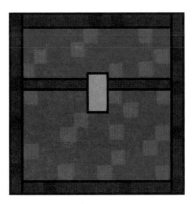

1. PEACEFUL TO GO A PLACE _Go to a peaceful place_

2. YOUR FEELINGS NAME _____

3. BREATHS THREE DEEP TAKE _____

4. A SAY MANTRA _____

5. BODY YOUR MELT _____

6. YOUR MOVE BODY _____

Read on to try these tricks, one by one.

A PEACEFUL PLACE

When your emotions grow stormy, it helps to retreat to a peaceful place. Where can you go when you want to be alone? To your bedroom? Into a cozy fort?

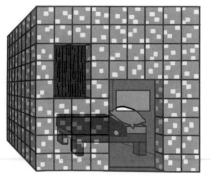

Name your peaceful place below, then think of some things you can keep there to help yourself feel better.

My peaceful place is_____.

HERE ARE THE THINGS I'LL KEEP THERE:

☐ Something that smells good, like lip balm or lotion

☐ Something that makes a peaceful sound

☐ Something I can touch, like a fidget toy

☐ Something warm and cozy, like a blanket

☐ Something I can hug, like a stuffed animal

☐ Something I can draw or write in, like a journal

☐ A picture or photo that makes me happy

Gather your items and check them off one by one.

PICTURE A PORTAL

If you can't go to a peaceful place, *imagine* it. Your mind is the portal that will take you there! Picture yourself on a sunny beach, in a beautiful meadow, or in your favorite Minecraft setting.

Tap into your senses to answer the questions below.

Where do you go? _____

What do you see there? _____

What do you smell? _____

What do you hear? _____

What do you feel under your feet? _____

Close your eyes again and imagine this place, using all of your senses to take you there.

DOODLE THE DETAILS

You can use a simple pencil to transport yourself to a place of peace when you need it. Adding details with colored pencils or crayons is even better to bring it to life!

Draw your peaceful place in the portal below.

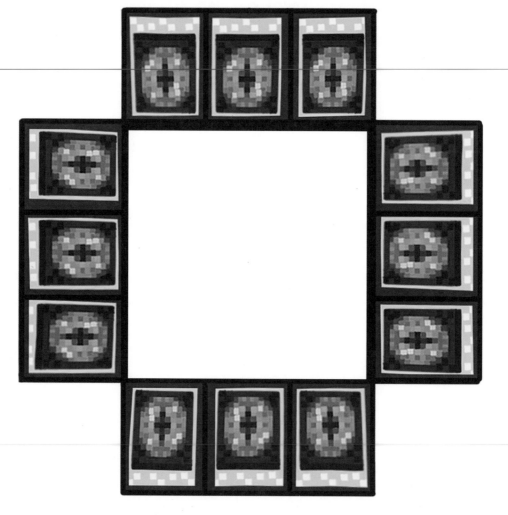

Whenever your emotions grow stormy, close your eyes and imagine stepping into the scene above.

FIND YOUR FEELINGS

When you're in a safe, quiet place, it's easier to figure out how you feel. What have you felt today?

Circle the emotions in the word puzzle below. Then draw a star next to the ones that you've felt today.

WORD LIST:

BORED

EXCITED

HAPPY

MAD

SAD

SCARED

STRESSED

SURPRISED

TIRED

WORRIED

E	X	C	I	T	E	D	S	O	S
I	F	R	L	E	C	B	T	O	U
V	U	H	A	P	P	Y	R	G	R
F	M	B	T	G	O	N	E	U	P
X	A	O	N	G	I	S	S	H	R
Z	D	R	F	W	T	E	S	O	I
G	S	E	A	T	I	R	E	D	S
S	P	D	S	D	F	J	D	R	E
E	A	O	W	O	R	R	I	E	D
D	A	D	S	C	A	R	E	D	B

EXAMINE THE EVIDENCE

Sometimes you're not sure *what* you're feeling, but your body gives you clues. Pretend you're a scientist studying the signs.

Follow the squiggly lines to match the clues your body gives with the emotions you might be feeling.

1. I have butterflies in my stomach.

2. My cheeks feel hot.

3. My hands are clenched into fists.

4. I have a lump in my throat.

5. My heart is racing.

A. **MAD**

B. **SCARED**

C. **SAD**

D. **NERVOUS**

E. **EMBARRASSED**

Everyone feels strong emotions a little bit differently. Read on to figure out how emotions feel for you.

COLOR YOUR MOOD

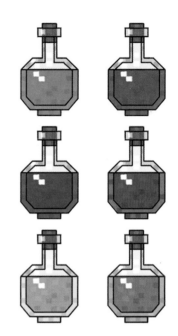

Color is another way to express how you feel. Do your emotions feel red hot? Cautious yellow? Calm, cool blue?

As you say each emotion out loud, close your eyes and picture a color. (*Hint:* There are no right or wrong answers!)

Use crayons or colored pencils to color in the potion bottles below.

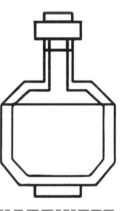

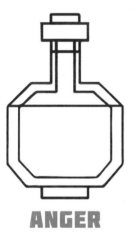

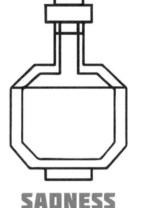

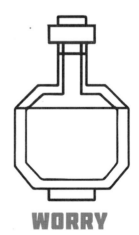

ANGER

SADNESS

HAPPINESS

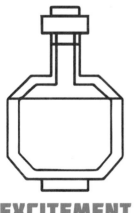

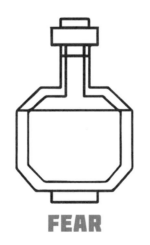

EXCITEMENT

FEAR

WORRY

LISTEN TO YOUR BREATH

Your breath gives you clues about how you're feeling. When you're scared or angry, you might breathe quickly through your mouth. Your chest might move up and down, as if you just ran a race.

Feel your breath right now. Put one hand on your chest and one hand on your belly. Take three breaths, and then answer the questions below.

Are you breathing fast or slow?_____

Which moves most: your chest or your belly?_____

Are you breathing through your nose or your mouth?_____

Based on these clues, how do you think you're feeling right now?

_____

Focusing on your breath helps you figure out how you feel. It can *also* help you feel better.

BLOCK BREATHS

Taking deep breaths can help you calm down. It's like giving your body and mind a mini time-out. Try a block breath using the Minecraft block below.

Slowly trace the block below with your finger, following the arrows and the instructions.

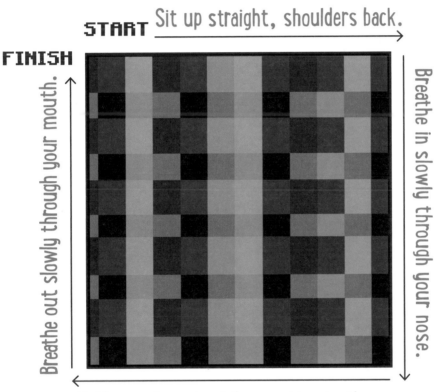

START — Sit up straight, shoulders back. →

FINISH

Breathe out slowly through your mouth.

Breathe in slowly through your nose.

← Hold your breath while counting to three.

Do a few block breaths any time you need to calm down. Trace an imaginary square with your finger or in your mind.

Name two places or times you could use block breathing.

1._____   2._____

MOUNTAIN BREATHS

To take deeper breaths, use your imagination. Inhale through your nose as you imagine scampering up a mountain like a goat. Exhale through your mouth as you imagine sliding down the other side.

Take five mountain breaths, coloring in one goat below after taking each breath.

Hint: Coloring can help you relax, too!

POWERFUL WORDS

A *mantra* is something we tell ourselves whenever we need help feeling strong. Which mantras could you use to handle big emotions?

Unscramble the words below to read each mantra.

❋ I am **G S T N O R** _____.

❋ I know what I'm **G F L E I E N** _____,
   and I know what to do.

❋ I can **A L H D N E** _____ big feelings.

❋ Feelings don't last. I won't **Y W A S L A** _____
   feel this way.

❋ I can help myself feel **T T R E B E** _____.

Which mantra is your favorite? Write it on a piece of paper and post it where you'll see it often.

MELT YOUR BODY

Just as taking deep breaths calms you down, relaxing your body does too. Imagine you are a snow golem that has wandered onto a hot, sandy beach.

Lie down and picture each body part melting into the sand, starting with your toes. Squeeze your toes for five seconds and then relax. Squeeze your legs for five seconds and then relax. Squeeze each body part, moving up to your arms, neck, and face.

Feel your whole body melt into the sand, and then answer these questions:

Which parts of your body were the hardest to "melt" or relax?

_____

How do you feel after your body melts?

_____

What details could you add the next time you "melt your body" on the beach? What could you imagine seeing, hearing, or feeling?

_____

MOVE LIKE A MOB

Some feelings, like boredom or worry, make it hard to sit still! When you're feeling that way, take a break and move your body. Try moving like your favorite mob or critter.

Unscramble the words below for different ways to move.

1. Bounce like a **L I M E S** _____

2. Teleport like an **M E R E A N D** _____

3. Creep like a **P R E S D I** _____

4. Run like a **F W L O** _____

5. Fly like an Ender **G A N R D O** _____

6. Stagger like a **B M O Z E I** _____

Can't decide which to try first? Roll a dice. Match the number you roll to the list above.

SHAKE IT OFF

Has anyone ever told you to "shake it off" when you get hurt or make a mistake? It means to let go and move on. Try this skeleton dance when you need to "shake off" tough emotions.

Shake each of these body parts as you count to 5. Check off the boxes below, one by one.

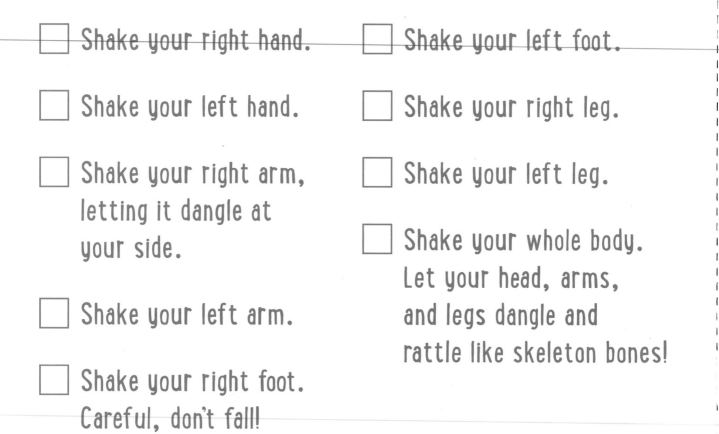

☐ Shake your right hand.

☐ Shake your left hand.

☐ Shake your right arm, letting it dangle at your side.

☐ Shake your left arm.

☐ Shake your right foot. Careful, don't fall!

☐ Shake your left foot.

☐ Shake your right leg.

☐ Shake your left leg.

☐ Shake your whole body. Let your head, arms, and legs dangle and rattle like skeleton bones!

Hint: Can't get up and dance because you're at school or out in public? Just shake your hands!

MORE FEEL-BETTER TRICKS

You've practiced some tricks for dealing with tough emotions. What else helps you feel better?

Circle one choice from each pair below.

Would you rather . . . ?

* Play with your pet   OR   Snuggle with a stuffed animal?

* Talk to a friend   OR   Talk to someone in your family?

* Take a warm bath   OR   Take a hot shower?

* Listen to music   OR   Read a book?

* Color a picture   OR   Squish some slime?

* Play a video game   OR   Play a board game?

* Watch a movie   OR   Step outside?

Figure out what helps *you* feel better, and add those things to your treasure chest of tricks.

SHINE YOUR LIGHT

Instead of focusing on dark feelings, shift your focus and think about something else. It's like holding a torch or flashlight. *You* get to decide where to shine your light.

Choose at least one of these tricks to try right now:

✳ **Focus on your breath.** Count your breaths up to 10. Count 1 as you inhale, 2 as you exhale, 3 as you inhale, and so on. If you lose count, start again.

✳ **Focus on your senses.** Name 3 things you can see right now, 2 things you can hear, and 1 thing you can feel.

✳ I can see_____, _____, and _____.

✳ I can hear_____, and _____.

✳ I can feel_____.

✳ **Focus on gratitude.** Name 3 people, places, or things you are thankful for.

1._____

2._____

3._____

See how much control you have over your thoughts? Don't dwell in dark places. Shine your light!

KNOW WHAT YOU NEED

Gardens in Minecraft need tending. Your emotions do too! When you're feeling a certain way, try to figure out what you need.

For each emotion below, think of one thing that might make you feel better.

Hint: If you get stuck, look back over the pages of this book.

When I feel bored, I might need to _____.

When I feel mad, I might need to _____.

When I feel frustrated, I might need to _____.

When I feel stressed, I might need to _____.

When I feel sad, I might need to _____.

Remember: Part of making good choices is figuring out what you need—and when.

MOOD METER

How can you spot anger before it strikes? Use a "mood meter." Just as you check your health meter in Minecraft, you can use a mood meter to check your feelings.

To finish this mood meter, add vowels (A, E, O, or U) in the blanks below.

6: ZAZADANGER! M _ L T D _ W N !

5: _ N G R Y ENOUGH TO CRY OR SHOUT

4: STARTING TO GET M _ D

3: FEELING F R _ S T R _ T _ D

2: A LITTLE _ N N _ Y _ D

1: C _ L M AND COOL

Copy the mood meter onto another sheet of paper. Post it on your bedroom door or mirror so that you can check your mood throughout the day, *before* you melt down.

WHEN STRONG FEELINGS STRIKE

Think of a few times when you felt strong emotions. When have you felt frustrated? Mad? Hurt?

Answer the questions below. Use the mood meter on the last page to rate your emotions from 1 to 6.

1. I felt_____when

_____.

   I was at a number_____on the mood meter.

2. I felt_____when

_____.

   I was at a number_____on the mood meter.

3. I felt_____when

_____.

   I was at a number_____on the mood meter.

MORE STORMY SITUATIONS

We all feel strong emotions in certain situations. When do *you* get upset most often?

Check all the statements below that sound like you.

I GET UPSET WHEN . . .

- [ ] I have to stop doing something fun.
- [ ] Someone won't let me sit with or play with them.
- [ ] I have to do homework or chores.
- [ ] I get a bad grade.
- [ ] I'm left out of something.
- [ ] Someone calls me a name or teases me.
- [ ] I mess up an assignment or a project.
- [ ] Someone won't share.
- [ ] Someone takes or breaks something of mine.
- [ ] I mess up in sports.

FEELINGS IN DISGUISE

Sometimes we act mad when we're actually feeling something else. What emotions could anger be covering up?

Draw a line to match the angry thoughts below with how you might *really* feel.

1. I'm mad that nobody wants to play with me.

2. I'm mad that I have to go to a new school.

3. I'm mad that my friend won't let me play their new video game.

4. I'm mad that the teacher scolded me.

A. I'm **jealous** because I don't have that game.

B. I'm **embarrassed** that I got scolded in front of the whole class.

C. I'm **sad** and **hurt** that no one wants to play with me.

D. I'm **scared** about going somewhere new.

The next time you feel angry, ask yourself, "Am I really mad, or am I feeling something else?"

ANGER CAN BEE OKAY

Sometimes anger can be helpful. Think of bees in Minecraft. They get angry when someone threatens their honey, right? When they buzz and swarm, it keeps their hive safe.

Can you help the bees get to their precious honey?

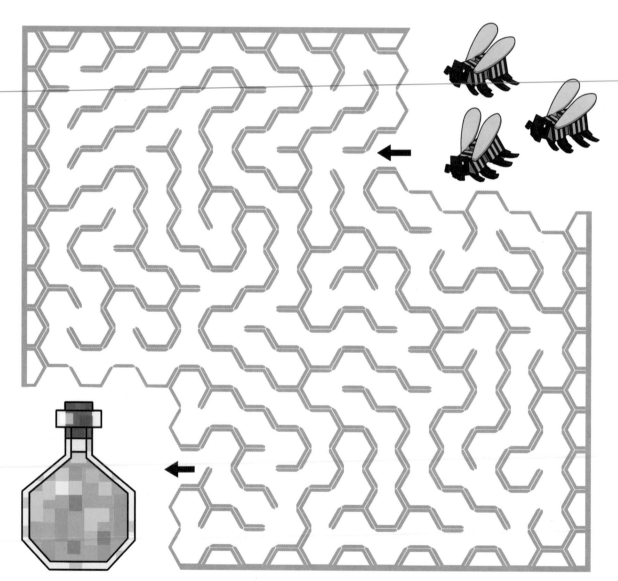

WHAT DO YOU STAND FOR?

Strong feelings can help you figure out who and what you care about most. When you feel scared or angry, you might be trying to protect yourself, your things, or the people and pets you care about.

Who and what do you stand up to protect? Fill in the blanks below.

I'll always stand up to protect my _____.

I get mad when someone says something mean about my

_____.

I don't like to share my _____ because I'm afraid it'll get broken.

I worry about my _____ getting lost or hurt.

The person I will always look out for is _____.

Remember: Strong feelings help us protect ourselves and the people and things we care about. But we can make a choice about how we express those feelings.

WHICH WAY?

There are good ways and not-so-good ways to express strong feelings. How do you know you're making a good choice?

To find out, circle each word that comes right after the word SIGN.

SIGN A IN APPLE SIGN GOOD BAD SIGN CHOICE THIS WAY SIGN MAKES CRAFTS MINES SIGN THINGS PEOPLE PLACES SIGN BETTER THAN THIS SIGN INSTEAD INSIDE BETWEEN SIGN OF OUT UP SIGN WORSE.

Write the words you circled here:

_____

_____

_____

_____

STOP AND THINK

When we're angry, it's normal to feel the urge to break something or hurt someone. But having a meltdown won't make things better. It'll only make things worse!

What can happen if we act on angry urges? Draw lines to match the choices below with something that might happen.

1. Threaten someone at school

2. Throw your phone or tablet

3. Hit your brother or sister

4. Slam your bedroom door

5. Call a friend a mean name

A. Scare a pet

B. Get it taken away

C. Get in trouble with a teacher

D. Lose or hurt that friend

E. Parents give you a time-out

Whenever you're about to act out your anger, ask yourself, "Will this choice make things better or worse?"

DANGER AHEAD!

It's easier to control your anger if you catch it early. How do you know when you're heading for a meltdown? Use your mood meter and listen to your body. It'll give you signs that there's danger ahead.

What warning signs does your body give? Check everything below that sounds like you.

☐ I feel shaky.

☐ My heart starts to pound.

☐ I feel like I'm going to be sick.

☐ My cheeks feel hot.

☐ I feel dizzy.

☐ I feel a rushing sound in my ears.

☐ My throat gets tight.

☐ I start breathing fast.

☐ I start to cry.

Spotting the signs of anger takes away some of its power. You know what your body is telling you, and you get to decide what happens next.

SLOW YOUR ROLL

When you feel a rush of anger, SLOW DOWN. Don't say or do anything that will make things worse. Count to 10 (or to 100, if you need to). *Then* decide what to do next.

Connect the dots below, 1 to 100, to discover another critter that moves slowly forward.

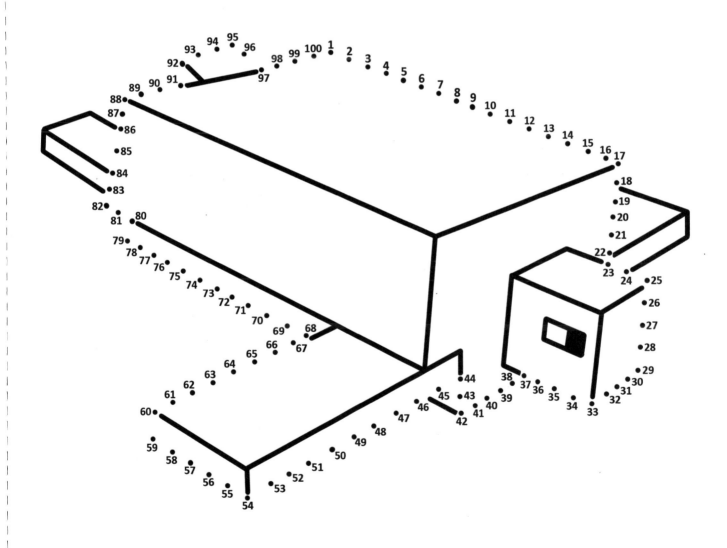

REMEMBER YOUR TREASURE CHEST

When anger strikes, remember the tricks you have in your treasure chest to help you calm down. Which of these could you try first? Second? Third?

Check your three favorite tricks from the list below.

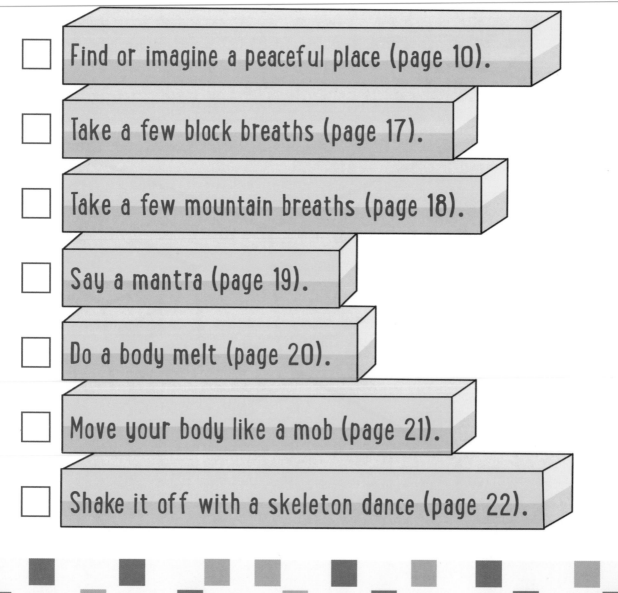

- ☐ Find or imagine a peaceful place (page 10).
- ☐ Take a few block breaths (page 17).
- ☐ Take a few mountain breaths (page 18).
- ☐ Say a mantra (page 19).
- ☐ Do a body melt (page 20).
- ☐ Move your body like a mob (page 21).
- ☐ Shake it off with a skeleton dance (page 22).

WALK AWAY—OR RUN

It isn't always easy to get away from a stressful situation. When you're away from home and can't go to your peaceful place, walk a few steps away to a quiet place.

Where could you go when anger strikes? Circle one choice in each line below.

1. If I'm in class when I get angry, I could . . .

   ask to go to the restroom   OR   sit at my desk and imagine a peaceful place

2. If I'm at a friend's house, I could ask to go . . .

   to the bathroom   OR   back home

3. If I'm at sports practice, I could ask to go . . .

   sit on the sidelines   OR   to the restroom

4. If I'm at recess, I could go . . .

   to a quiet part of the playground   OR   to stand near the playground monitor

There are no right or wrong answers. But if you plan ahead for a quiet place to go, you'll be ready to handle strong feelings—no matter where you are.

CARRY CALM WITH YOU

What if you could take your peaceful place with you on the go? You can!

Pack a small bag with a few feel-good things, just like the ones you keep in your peaceful place at home.

HERE ARE THE THINGS I'LL PACK:

- [ ] Something that smells good, like lip balm or travel-sized lotion

- [ ] Something I can draw or write in, like a journal

- [ ] Something I can touch, like a fidget toy

- [ ] A picture or photo that makes me happy

- [ ] Something warm and cozy, like a tiny stuffed animal

As you pack your items in a backpack or bag, check them off one by one.

COLOR BREATHS

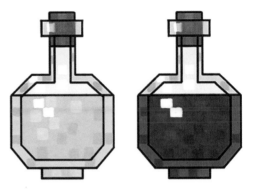

Remember the colors you chose to express your many moods? (Turn back to page 15 for a reminder.) Imagine that you could breathe in a calm color like blue and breathe out your red-hot anger.

Take five color breaths, inhaling calm and exhaling anger. Color in one potion bottle below after taking each breath.

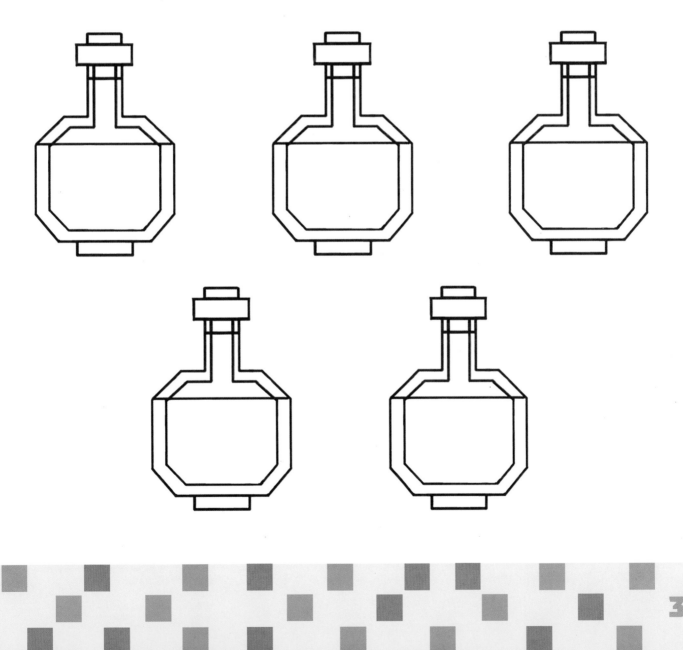

SNOWBALL SQUEEZES

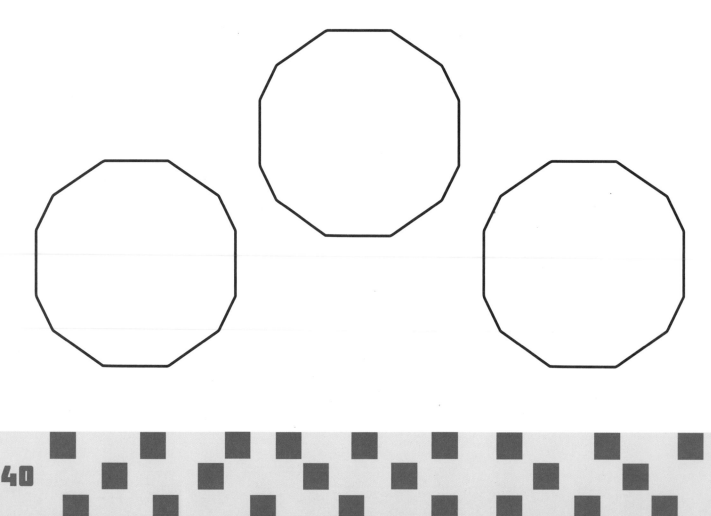

It's hard to lie down and do full body melts when you're away from home. Instead of squeezing and melting your whole "snow golem" body, try snowball squeezes.

Clench your hands into fists as if you're crushing snowballs. Count to 5 and then release, letting your hands and fingers melt down into your lap.

You can do snowball squeezes *anywhere* when you need to calm down.

Where could you try them? Write three places in the snowballs below.

FACE YOUR FEELINGS

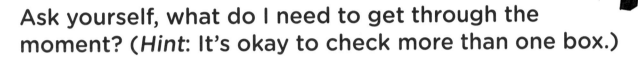

Facing your feelings means figuring out what you feel and what you need. Can you remember a time when your emotions felt stormy? Use your imagination to "teleport" back to that moment, like an Enderman.

Ask yourself, what do I need to get through the moment? (*Hint*: It's okay to check more than one box.)

☐ A hug

☐ An apology

☐ Help with an assignment

☐ A snack

☐ Something fun to do

☐ To be included

☐ To make my own choice

☐ A little encouragement

☐ Some alone time

☐ To move my body

☐ To get more sleep

☐ A friend to talk with or sit by

☐ To protect someone or something

☐ More time to finish

Once you figure out what you need, you can make a good choice about how to ask for it.

REQUESTS VERSUS DEMANDS

Asking for what you need is better than demanding it. Demands are like fireballs. Other people will want to dodge them, or fire back. Can you tell the difference between requests and demands?

Circle one answer in each line below.

1. "Give that back!"   REQUEST OR **DEMAND**

2. "Could you be more gentle with that, please?"   REQUEST OR **DEMAND**

3. "May I play, too?"   REQUEST OR **DEMAND**

4. "Stop bothering me!"   REQUEST OR **DEMAND**

5. "Say you're sorry!"   REQUEST OR **DEMAND**

6. "Is it my turn next?"   REQUEST OR **DEMAND**

7. "Don't break that!"   REQUEST OR **DEMAND**

8. "Could I have a little more time?"   REQUEST OR **DEMAND**

9. "No fair—let me pick this time!"   REQUEST OR **DEMAND**

PICK YOUR PATH

Remember: Your feelings don't control you. YOU get to choose how to react to them. You decide which path you'll take and what happens next.

Can you find your way to feeling better? Choose path 1, 2, or 3 below.

1
2
3

MAKING MISTAKES

Everyone makes mistakes—in mazes, in Minecraft, and in real life. If you get angry and do something you regret, be kind to yourself. You're still learning how to be the boss of your behavior. It takes time!

Think of a time when you got angry, and you did or said something you regret. Fill in the blanks below.

❋ A time I felt angry: _____

_____ .

❋ Here's what I did: _____

_____ .

❋ Here's what happened next: _____

_____ .

❋ Here's what I *wish* I had done instead: _____

_____

_____ .

BE KIND TO YOURSELF

If a friend messed up, you'd give them a hug and say something nice, right? Treat yourself the same way! If you make a mistake, give yourself a hug and say something kind.

To find some reassuring words to use, circle every word that comes right after the word FRIEND.

FRIEND WE YOU ME FRIEND ALL EVERYONE FRIEND MAKE MINE CRAFT FRIEND MISTAKES FRIEND BUT OR FOR FRIEND WE ME US FRIEND CAN CAN'T FRIEND DO DUE DEW FRIEND THINGS PLACES PEOPLE FRIEND DIFFERENTLY OR THE SAME FRIEND NEXT LAST FIRST FRIEND TIME.

Write the words you circled here:

_____

_____

_____

_____

SAY "SORRY"

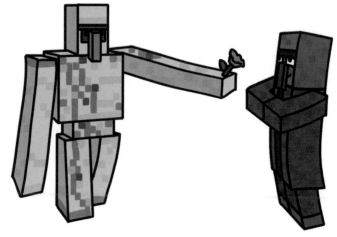

If you do something you regret, say you're sorry—even if it it's hard. Apologizing will help you set things right.

Think of a time when you had a meltdown and hurt someone's feelings. What words could you have used to apologize? Start with the words below, and fill in the blanks.

I'm sorry that I _____

_____

_____ .

I wish I hadn't done that. Next time, I will try to _____

_____

_____ .

WHERE DO STORMS STRIKE?

If you want to do things differently next time, you have to be prepared for stormy feelings. Try to spot the places where anger might strike.

Where do you get mad the most often?
Check off those places below.

☐ At home

☐ In class

☐ At recess

☐ At the doctor
  or dentist

☐ In the car

☐ At a store

☐ Waiting in line

☐ At a friend's house

☐ Somewhere else: _____

_____

_____

_____

MAKE A PLAN

Pick one of the places you chose on the last page, and think about a time you got angry there. What could you do if it happens again?

To make a plan for next time, fill in the blanks below.

Where I was: _____

_____

What happened: _____

_____

What I needed: _____

_____

Something I could do or bring with me *next* time: _____

_____

WATCH FOR TRIP WIRES

In Minecraft, a trip wire is like a trap. In real life, there are "trip wires" that can lead to stormy feelings. Do you know what some of those are?

To find out, unscramble the words below.

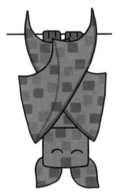

1. Feeling **D T R E I** _____

2. Feeling **G Y R U H N** _____

3. Feeling **R D B E O** _____

DON'T BE CAUGHT OFF GUARD

When do you often feel hungry, tired, or bored? If you know when you might feel that way, you won't be caught by surprise, and you can start to plan ahead.

Fill in the blanks below.

I sometimes get hangry (hungry and angry) when I'm at

_____ or at _____.

I get so tired at _____ and at _____

that I start feeling crabby.

When I get bored at _____ or at _____,

I start heading for a meltdown.

Read on for ways to plan ahead—and to stop a meltdown before it starts.

PLAN FOR SNACK ATTACKS

If you're heading somewhere you know you'll be hungry, like for a long car ride or to sports practice after school, pack a snack.

Think of one healthy snack you can pack for every color of the rainbow.

Red: _____

Orange: _____

Yellow: _____

Green: _____

Blue: _____

Purple: _____

DON'T BE A ZOMBIE

Get the sleep you need! That's the best way to avoid feeling tired—and crabby—throughout the day.

Check the statements below that are true about your sleep routine.

☐ I don't drink soda or hot chocolate at night.

☐ I go to bed at about the same time every night.

☐ I sleep 9 or 10 hours most nights.

☐ I try to move my body (at recess or in sports) for at least an hour every day.

☐ I put away phones, tablets, and video games at least an hour before bedtime.

For every check you made above, color in two hearts below.

Is your health meter full? If not, choose another healthy habit to add to your sleep routine. Put a star next to something you could try.

BOREDOM BUSTERS

If boredom brings your mood down, plan ahead. Pack boredom busters in your backpack before you head out the door, or keep them in a bin in your room.

Circle the boredom busters in the word puzzle below.

WORD LIST:

BOOKS

CARDS

CRAYONS

FIDGET TOYS

GAMES

MUSIC

NOTEBOOK

SKETCHPAD

SNACKS

B	F	C	M	G	A	M	E	S	I
N	I	S	R	U	H	F	I	B	C
C	D	K	O	A	S	O	O	O	N
A	G	E	K	B	Y	I	Q	O	O
R	E	T	A	R	G	O	C	K	T
D	T	C	V	Z	G	A	N	S	E
S	T	H	S	N	A	C	K	S	B
T	O	P	M	H	R	S	F	H	O
Z	Y	A	D	E	B	G	T	N	O
P	S	D	O	D	C	Y	U	P	K

THE BLAME GAME

"She made me mad!" "He made me do that!" Have you ever said those things? We all have! But the truth is, no one else can *make* you do something. Remember: You're the boss of your own behavior.

Unscramble the words below for more good reminders.

1. You get to **E O C O H S** _____ how much you'll let someone **R E B T O H** _____ you.

2. You can't control how other people **E T A R T** _____ you, but you **C N A** _____ control what you say or do.

3. You get to choose how you'll **C A T R E** _____ to their words or actions.

GETTING ALONG

We all have to deal with difficult people sometimes. If someone is mean to you, you might want to be mean back. But will that make things better? Nope. Before you react, think things through.

Think of someone you have trouble getting along with, and then fill in the blanks below.

1. What they do: _____
   _____

2. How you feel when it happens: _____
   _____

3. How you react: _____
   _____

4. What you need or wish they would do instead: _____
   _____

IN THEIR SHOES

When someone says or does something that frustrates you, try to put yourself in their shoes. Everyone you meet has feelings and needs, just like you. Try to figure out what those are.

Draw a line between the people below and the needs they might have.

1. Mom or Dad hollers because you didn't clean your room.

A. They need a turn or to feel included.

2. Your teacher scolds you for talking in class.

B. They need help keeping the house clean.

3. Your little brother or sister steals your game controller.

C. They need to manage the classroom so that everyone can learn.

Making good choices is about figuring out what you need *and* what other people might need.

YOUR NEEDS, THEIR NEEDS

Everyone is different. What you want and need might be different from what other people want and need—and that's okay!

Which of these would you rather do? Circle your choices, and have a friend circle their choices with a different colored pencil or pen.

Would you rather . . .

1. Do homework with a study buddy   OR   Study by yourself?

2. Be a team captain   OR   Be chosen as part of the team?

3. Decide what to play   OR   Have someone else come up with ideas?

4. Share snacks   OR   Each have your own snacks?

5. Have a sleepover every weekend   OR   Have a sleepover once in a while?

6. Play with one friend   OR   Play with a group of friends?

Did you and your friend choose different answers? Good! Talk about why. And remember—it's okay to like, want, and need different things.

I FEEL . . . WHEN YOU . . .

No one can read your mind. If you need something from someone, ask for it nicely—*before* you get angry. Follow these steps for saying how you feel and what you need.

Step 1: Start with the words "I feel . . ."

Step 2: Add "when you . . ." Be specific—but not mean—about something the person is doing that upsets you.

Step 3: Finish with "I would like for you to . . ." What do you wish this person would do differently?

Practice the words below. Think of something a friend is doing that hurts you. Can you let them know how you feel?

I feel _____ when you _____

_____. I would like for you to _____

_____

_____ .

BREW A HEALING POTION

Can you give *yourself* what you need? Absolutely! When you're feeling stormy, imagine that you can brew a healing potion that will help you feel better.

What would you put in it? Add the following ingredients, filling in the blanks below.

One thing I might need: _____

One place I can go (or imagine going): _____

One thing I can do: _____

Someone I can talk to: _____

Something I can tell myself: _____

After trying the tricks in this book, you have *all* the ingredients you need to tackle tough emotions and make good choices.

POST A REMINDER

Trace the sign below on another piece of paper. Decorate it and post it where you'll see it often, such as on your bedroom door or bathroom mirror.

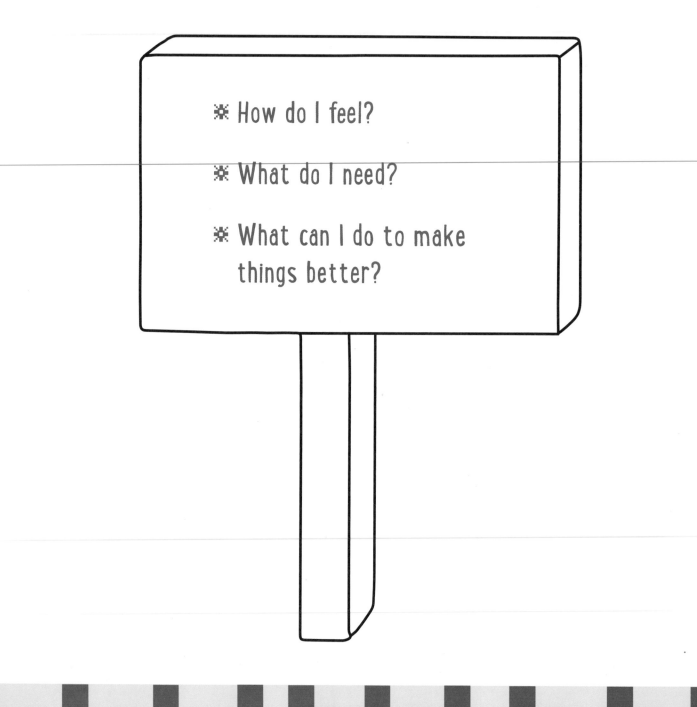

✳ How do I feel?

✳ What do I need?

✳ What can I do to make things better?

Whenever you see your sign, check in with your feelings.

You know how to spot stormy feelings.
You know how to ask for what you need.
And you know how to make things better.

You've got this!

ANSWER KEY

Page 8

YOU CAN CONTROL HOW YOU ACT ON YOUR FEELINGS. YOU'RE THE BOSS OF YOUR BEHAVIOR.

Page 9

1. GO TO A PEACEFUL PLACE.
2. NAME YOUR FEELINGS.
3. TAKE THREE DEEP BREATHS.
4. SAY A MANTRA.
5. MELT YOUR BODY.
6. MOVE YOUR BODY.

Page 13

Page 14

1. D
2. E
3. A
4. C
5. B

Page 19

STRONG

FEELING

HANDLE

ALWAYS

BETTER

Page 21

1. SLIME
2. ENDERMAN
3. SPIDER
4. WOLF
5. DRAGON
6. ZOMBIE

Page 26

6: MELTDOWN

5: ANGRY

4: MAD

3: FRUSTRATED

2: ANNOYED

1: CALM

Page 29

1. C
2. D
3. A
4. B

Page 30

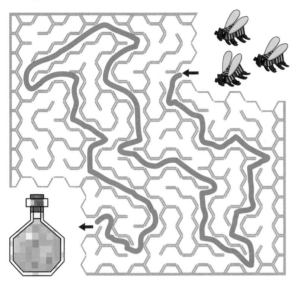

Page 32

A GOOD CHOICE MAKES THINGS BETTER INSTEAD OF WORSE.

Page 33

1. C
2. B
3. E
4. A
5. D

Page 35

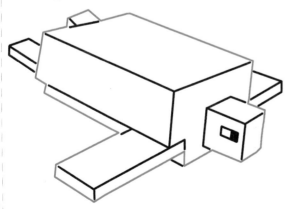

Page 42

1. DEMAND
2. REQUEST
3. REQUEST
4. DEMAND
5. DEMAND
6. REQUEST
7. DEMAND
8. REQUEST
9. DEMAND

Page 43

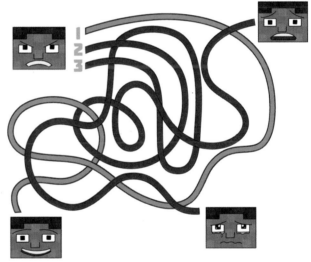

PATH #1

Page 45

WE ALL MAKE MISTAKES BUT WE CAN DO THINGS DIFFERENTLY NEXT TIME.

Page 49

1. TIRED
2. HUNGRY
3. BORED

Page 53

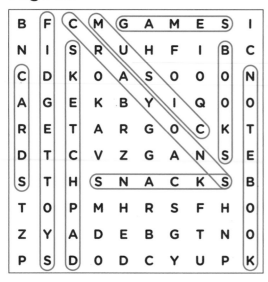

Page 54

1. YOU GET TO **CHOOSE** HOW MUCH YOU'LL LET SOMEONE **BOTHER** YOU.

2. YOU CAN'T CONTROL HOW OTHER PEOPLE **TREAT** YOU, BUT YOU **CAN** CONTROL WHAT YOU SAY OR DO.

3. YOU GET TO CHOOSE HOW YOU'LL **REACT** TO THEIR WORDS OR ACTIONS.

Page 56

1. B
2. C
3. A